Making Up Stories

with children

Alison Shakspeare

Text © Alison Shakspeare 2010

First published 2010 by **Southgate Publishers Ltd**

The Square, Sandford, Crediton, Devon EX17 4LW

www.southgatepublishers.co.uk

Printed and bound in Great Britain by HSW Print, Tonypandy, Rhondda, Wales

British Library Cataloguing in Publication Data

A CIP catalogue record for this book is available from the British Library.

ISBN 9 781857 411379

Acknowledgements

Illustrated by Clare Elsom

Designed by Daniel Loveday

Thanks to the following for their help, advice and encouragement: Crediton Children's Centre and Devon Family Learning; Sean Alexander; Tony, Sharon and Jessica; Charlie Werner; Geoff Fox; Don Newton; and VJ.

Contents

I can't make up stories!   4

Where are the ideas going
to come from?   5

Be prepared   8

Key points to a story   14

    Who   15

    Where   16

    When   17

    What   18

    Why   19

Getting started   20

Keeping a record   23

Useful resources   24

I can't make up stories!

If you feel this way then this is the booklet for you. On every page you will find some basic ideas to get you started and keep you going. At the heart of it all is sharing the experience with your child and making the stories belong to the family.

These are some of the reasons why it is worth making up your own stories:

- it's great fun and can be exciting
- you and your child will benefit from spending time together
- it stimulates your child's imagination
- it helps them to understand the world and how it works
- it develops their listening and language skills
- you share memories, which helps them identify who they are and where they come from
- you help them to build pictures in their minds

Where are the ideas going to come from?

Life's a tale

Just the smallest thing about where you live or the tiniest event in the daily life of any member of your family can be a starting point. You'll be in good company. Many classic children's stories started life in this way. Winnie the Pooh was a soft toy given to the family; Beatrix Potter's animal tales came from live animals she owned; The Wind in the Willows and Watership Down were inspired by landscapes.

Think about your life or what you've heard from older relatives, your childhood, chats you've had with friends, events your child has been involved in or is worried about. They could all be the start of a story – and they are already in your head. With the help of the following pages you can turn them into a story to share with your child.

Once upon a time

You could think back to a traditional tale you were told as a child, to a pantomime you went to one Christmas or a character in that favourite DVD your child has sat through a hundred times. Then use it as a skeleton or starting point for your own story.

There is a reason fairy stories, myths and legends keep being retold: they teach us something about who we are and why we do things; they keep us in touch with our culture and tradition; the basic structure makes them easy to remember and follow. That's why they get adapted for pantomime and why Disney turned them into cartoons.

Even by retelling an old favourite you'll be:

- passing on to your child classic tales which will help them to understand the books and films they'll come across later on
- helping your child appreciate their own heritage and that of others

Suggestions

⭐ *a search on the internet under storytelling, myths or legends will lead you to more story ideas than you'll ever have the time to tell;*

⭐ *refresh your memory with a re-read of myths and legends from a book borrowed from your local library.*

You're not alone

In fact the whole point is that it's not just you. Your greatest help and inspiration will be sitting right beside you. You can create a magical experience by connecting your personal experience to your child's imagination, dreams and reactions.

So it is really important that you actively involve your child as often as you can. Ask them for their ideas and suggestions. But you must listen to what they say and use those ideas, however crazy - you never know what magic might happen.

Suggestions

⭐ *use a story to help your child deal with an emotional experience like a death in the family or being bullied;*

⭐ *use a story to introduce a new event, such as starting school or going into hospital.*

Be prepared

Time and place

Can you create a special story place? Is there a cosy corner where you can be comfortable and reasonably quiet? You want as few distractions from the television, the telephone and other people as possible.

A great time for a good story is bedtime. But don't make it all too exciting and noisy or you'll be waking them up, not helping them to sleep. If you can give yourself about twenty clear minutes you won't feel rushed and neither will you feel you have to go on for longer than you can cope with.

However, there are plenty of other times that are great for stories - when you are on a long journey or a day out, at a picnic or on a beach. They're good opportunites for an exciting adventure story.

Suggestions

★ use your surroundings as an inspiration for your story. Perhaps bath time suggests a beach story;

★ what season is it? Pouring rain or a fall of snow can add atmosphere and make you feel all snug indoors;

★ a blazing hot holiday might make you think of pirates and a treasure hunt.

A treasure sack…

… or box or drawer or shelf. Whether your imagination is raring to go or not, a few props are always handy, especially if this is all new to you. Gather a few objects together that will help fire everybody's imagination when you need to make a decision about the key points of your story.

A favourite soft toy or doll could become the central character in a whole series of stories or an ongoing adventure. Or, used like a puppet, it could act as the storyteller. This is particularly useful if you are dealing with a story that touches on a difficult experience your child is having.

Build up a hoard of 'treasures': bits of jewellery, colourful pebbles, strange shaped bits of wood, old photos, little statuettes, miniatures of everyday objects. When you are collecting your hoard, how about involving other family members? Ask them to contribute to the 'treasure' with some extra surprises.

Your child might like to make their own collection of favourite toys. Then you can weave them together into a story.

Then, when you need to decide on a *who* or a *what*, you can ask your child to choose an object from the treasure sack. Make it more fun by asking them to close their eyes and take one out at random.

Questions to ask your child about the 'treasure'

★ what name shall she/he/it have?

★ what magic thing can this rock/bangle/scarf do?

★ where does this ball/elephant/vase live?

★ why not make a treasure holder together?
  Decorate a shoe box or sew shapes onto
  a PE bag.

Be positive

However you feel at least pretend you're confident! Relax and smile. Don't apologise as you start, either with words or with your body language. Remember, it's not a test; it's a bit of fun.

If you are hesitant or anxious, you'll be boring and unappealing. To hold your child's attention:

- sit comfortably and cosily
- use a variety of voices and speak both loudly and softly
- change the pace as the story changes, be energetic, then be still and silent

Treat your voice well:

- breathe deeply but naturally so you have plenty of puff
- relax your throat, neck and shoulder muscles
- speak clearly

If you can 'see' the story in your head you will feel involved and it will be easier to involve your child.

Keep the flow going

Be flexible. If your child suggests something, which may change a plot or ending you'd already decided on, be positive about using it. At least discuss it; don't just ignore it. It's both your imaginations that are being stimulated.

Perhaps you are making up stories with more than one child or you have a child who constantly interrupts. Then, to keep the flow of the story going, it can help to establish a few ground rules, such as:

- only one person talks at a time, then everybody gets heard
- take it in turns to decide what happens next, then everybody gets a go
- once part of a story has been decided it can only be changed if everybody agrees to it

Key points to a story

There are five key points to any good story. You can decide on them in any order and don't worry about deciding on them all before you start. You can allow them to develop as you go along.

The next pages will give you some ideas on each key point and how to use them. They are:

★ **Who**

★ **Where**

★ **When**

★ **What**

★ **Why**

★ To help you remember, why not write each of these key points on a separate piece of card and stick them up where you can see them?

★ Make them different from each other by using different colours, or drawing or sticking a little picture on each one.

Who

You need a central figure for your story. They could be:

- a person (your child, a fantasy figure or a historical character)
- an animal (a favourite soft toy or a family pet)
- a thing (a machine, a toy, a tree or even a shop or lighthouse)

If you can't decide on one then use your treasure sack. Ask your child to shut their eyes and pull something out of your treasure sack – just like the nursery rhyme about Little Jack Horner:

"He put in his thumb
and pulled out a plum!"

Together decide on a name for your central figure and talk about what he/she/it looks like and can do. Ask your child questions:

- Is it huge or tiny?
- Is she blue or black or green with red spots?
- Is he just ordinary or can he change shape or grant wishes?

Are you going to tell the story as though you were the central character? *"I went into the cave and saw the giant dragon."* Or are you telling the story on behalf of the character (who might be your child)? *"So then you decided to follow the path."* Or the character might be someone else: *"Then Bertie Bear leapt up into the tree."*

If you and your child like this character, then keep on using them to help you both remember your stories. Build up a series of adventures and develop what they can do and what they learn from event to event. If your child wants to hear a particular story again, then ask them to start telling more and more of it themselves, even if they change bits!

Suggestions

- a grandma who can do magic;
- a cat that fits through any space;
- a bus that can fly.

Where

Choose somewhere for your story to take place. You might feel more comfortable with a place you know, such as your own house or street or the local shopping centre.

But if your tale needs somewhere more magical then go for it! Even if you start the tale in the bedroom a cupboard or a mirror can then become the doorway to the next place - a forest, a town, an island, a factory, a ship, a castle, a jet plane or rocket.

Remember, you don't have to plan everything in advance. Just like a journey, let it unfold step by step.

Suggestions
- *an island that moves about;*
- *a fire station with a magic pole;*
- *a track through a forest.*

When

Is your story going to take place in the past, the present or the future? Perhaps you could do some time travelling.

Don't worry about the actual date you are talking about but think about how much life has changed in the last 100 years and how that affects behaviour:

- The modern car engine didn't exist before 1885 – think how much faster you can get about by car than on horseback or on foot.
- Personal computers have only been available since 1977 – now you can find out so much, so quickly, by using the internet.
- Once upon a time you had to go through an operator to make a telephone call. Now almost everyone has a mobile phone – what a difference that makes to keeping in touch or calling for help.

Children love hearing about things that link to their own family's past. A family member's contribution to your treasure sack could help you remember something that happened to you as a child or a piece of family history that you can retell. Maybe you got lost once and then you were found; perhaps you experienced a holiday adventure in a foreign place. You could even use a wartime tale from a grandparent's childhood.

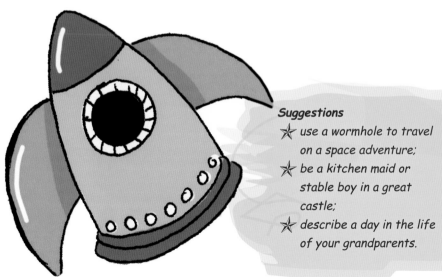

Suggestions
- ⭐ *use a wormhole to travel on a space adventure;*
- ⭐ *be a kitchen maid or stable boy in a great castle;*
- ⭐ *describe a day in the life of your grandparents.*

What

What is your main character looking for, or are they hiding something? Do they need to get something to somebody? Maybe that something is magical or precious; maybe it always tells the truth or makes people feel better.

This is another good time to use your treasure sack. A piece of jewellery can be something precious; a bit of cloth may well be some magic clothing; a strangely shaped stone or a little jar might grant wishes.

> **Suggestions**
> ★ a cloak of invisibility;
> ★ a chest full of gold;
> ★ a Wii that tells the future.

Why ?

This is the bit that turns a description into an adventure. Ask why the character is doing what they are doing, what is their job or the aim of the story? What is their effect on other people, or how do other people affect them? A good adventure can often mean beating a baddie.

Is there something your main character has to find out? Is something nasty about to happen that they can stop? Do they have to achieve something to make their life better?

Perhaps somebody had to move from the family home to a completely new country because of a war or because they needed to find work or to look for a lost person.

Suggestions
- ⭐ to stop a fox eating the chickens;
- ⭐ to find a friend lost in a cave;
- ⭐ to become the best in the football team.

Getting started

Here are some short examples to help you and your child get started on a fun and magical journey.

Joining toys together

If you've asked your child to put some favourite toys into a treasure sack, how are you going to work a story around them? You may end up with more than one story. For instance out of a plane, a flying dinosaur, a jumping frog, a scooter, a medal, a triceratops, a fish and a shell the following stories can be told:

- ✶ The plane helped the flying dinosaur find its favourite food. They flew over rivers and mountains and forests. The dinosaur (played by the child) said no to lots of food (fish, sheep and fruit) and a big yes to its favourite (sweetcorn) growing in a field at the end of the journey.
- ✶ The frog rode its scooter alongside the child who wanted to enter the school sports day but whose feet hurt. So the frog led the child down a road and through a wood to a shallow pond. After paddling in the magic water the child went back to the school and ran such a fast race that he won the medal.
- ✶ The stomping triceratops was bellowing miserably by the seashore because he had lost his family. The fish brought him the magic shell which told him how to find his family. He followed the instructions and they were all happily brought together again.

There are many opportunities in each of those stories for you to use different voices, show happy and sad faces and give longer or shorter descriptions of places. You can say lots about why things have happened. You can also get your child to move the toys as the story goes along and to play one of the characters.

A fairy story

Key point	Story skeleton	Filling in the gaps	Ask your child
When	One night, many years ago, at the end of the day	What season was it? What was the weather doing?	
Who	A couple	Describe them: age, hair colour, relationship.	What names should they have?
Where	Sat in their kitchen	Can you describe the kitchen?	
What	Moaning and groaning about how small their house was, how slow their old car was, how tatty their clothes were.	What other things can they moan about? What neighbour's possession might they want? Use a deeper voice for him and a higher voice for her.	
Who	A fairy appears	Describe her: size, colour, clothes, accessories. Does she appear on the table, in the fireplace or hovering?	
Why	The fairy has heard their moaning and gives them three wishes as a test: one for him, one for her, one joint one.	What sort of voice would she speak in?	What might the wishes be?
When	The fairy gives them some time to decide on the wishes.	How long do they have?	
Why	They start to argue about what they want. Then the woman 'wishes' she had a sausage – and it appears. He is so cross at a wasted wish he 'wishes' it was on her nose! That leaves them one wish! Finally they see the only solution is to wish to be just as they were before – which wasn't so bad after all.	What sort of wishes would they argue about? Make her voice all bunged up when she has the sausage on her nose.	Talk about the good things in your life.

The day the car broke down

⭐ **Where** were you going when you went out to the car? Was it a boring job you had to do; an urgent appointment you had to keep; a treat you were going on?

⭐ **Who** had to get there? Was it just one of you; the whole family; a friend, neighbour or someone else?

⭐ **What** did you do instead? Did you go to a neighbour; catch a bus; call a family member; get offered a ride in a magic carriage/rocket/balloon?

⭐ **Why** did the ride turn into an adventure? Was it because you met new people; went to strange places; did a spot of time-travelling; found something that had been lost?

⭐ **When** did you get back, if ever?

Another day at work or play

⭐ Somebody goes to school/work every day and every day they do the same thing. Perhaps they have a special place they go to when it all gets too much – behind a bush or in a cupboard.

⭐ One day they find a pen on the floor/their desk/in their special place. Or perhaps they are given the pen by a strange creature.

⭐ When they use the pen to draw a picture or write a wish it comes true.

⭐ What adventures do they have? Perhaps they go into another world; face up to a bully, take a difficult exam; discover a way to make a fantastic new tool or toy.

Keeping a record

Why not hang on to your own stories? Then you can:

- tell your favourites again and again
- keep track of characters and story lines
- hold on to the memories of a wonderful time

Also, your child could use them if you can't be there for any reason.

There are several ways to record your stories depending on whether you want to:

- do it during storytime or afterwards
- do it with paints and crayons or glue and pictures
- write it all down and develop it
- do it together or alone

Live recording

Audio or video recording is the easy way to make an instant record at the same time as you are making up your stories. You don't even need a video camera or dictaphone since mobile phones and digital cameras can be used to make short recordings.

Once you've done your recording you could just play it again and delete it. Or you could transfer it to a DVD or as a file on a computer so that you can replay it. Or you could use it as a memory jogger to make a scrapbook or notebook.

Story scrapbook

Creating a scrapbook is a great next step in developing skills as well as a perfect occupation for your child (preferably with, but even without, you). Get out a blank sheet of paper or buy a scrapbook or create a file. Then with pencils, paint, glue and shapes, get drawing, sticking, writing and recreate or develop the story.

Notebook

You could write down your stories either as a series of notes or out in full. If you can't manage the time straight after the story session you could use the recording or the scrapbook as a reminder.

You could then develop the stories and, if you like to draw, you could also do some illustrations.

Useful resources

Once you've started finding and telling your stories we hope you will share them with us on www.makingupstories.co.uk

You can type in your ideas and stories, upload your videos and see what others are doing.

Society for Storytelling for anyone with an interest in oral storytelling, whether teller, listener, beginner or professional – http://sfs.org.uk

StoryBee, where you can listen to professional storytellers spinning their wonderful tales – www.storybee.org

Storyshapes sell tactile prompts as reminders of the key elements of a story – www.storyshapes.com

SurLaLune Fairy Tales features annotated fairy tales, their histories, similar tales across cultures and modern interpretations – www.surlalunefairytales.com

The National Literacy Trust is an independent charity that changes lives through literacy – www.literacytrust.org.uk

Your local library may run storytelling sessions and that's where you can find books to help with ideas.

Other booklets for parents and families published by Southgate:

How to Enjoy Reading Aloud to Young Children is a different kind of booklet for parents about reading with expression and confidence. It makes sharing books with children much more rewarding and enjoyable for both adult and child. It is full of easy-to-follow techniques and advice using short extracts from well-loved children's stories.

- Bullying: A Guide for Parents
- Dad Did It!
- Five-a-day Pro
- Hot Tips for a Cool Planet
- Living with Your Adolescent
- Lunchbox Pro
- Managing Difficult Behaviour
- The Numbers Game

www.southgatepublishers.co.uk